Glass Flowers

Glass Flowers

Diane Fahey

PUNCHER & WATTMANN

First published in 2021
Published by Puncher and Wattmann
PO Box 279
Waratah NSW 2298

http://www.puncherandwattmann.com
puncherandwattmann@bigpond.com

ISBN   9781922571137

Cover image © Dena Kahan, *Large Glass Garden #2*
Cover design by Miranda Douglas
Typesetting by Morgan Arnett
Printed by Lightning Source International

A catalogue record for this book is available from the National Library of Australia

NATIONAL
LIBRARY
OF AUSTRALIA

Contents

The Silver Garden

Blackout	9
Unearthly	12
Autumn Begins	14
'A History of the Lotus'	16
Late Spring Gardens	18
Cloud Life	21
Introit	22
After Rain	24
Blackbird	26
Garden Walk, Daybreak	29
The Unquiet Garden	32
Zen Morning	34
The White Cockatoos	36
Visitations	38
Summer Poem	40
At the Solstice	42
Midsummer	44
Late Summer Sea	46
Anniversary Visit	48
Bowers	49
In Winter Light	52

In Silent Rooms

Glass Flowers	57
The Yellow Room	62

Face   64
  In Silent Rooms   64
  Portrait in the mirror   65
  Dressing table (self portrait)   66
  Coda   68
The Black Cockatoos   69
Portraiture   74
  Au Tambour, 63 quai de la Tournelle (5e arr.), 1908   74
  Boutique empire, rue du Faubourg-Saint-Honoré, 1902   75
  The Square   75
At Niagara Galleries   77
The Postcard   82
The Room   87
Rooms by the Sea   90
Lake with Moonlight   92
Flight to the Stars   95
  At the Archibald Portrait Prize, 2017   95
Shimmer   98
  Nothing but Stars   98
  A Ceiling in Paris   99
  Djotarra Dying   100
  Her Blessing   101
Dancer   102
Shadows   106
  St. Peter Healing the Sick with His Shadow by Masaccio 106
  Intensive Care: COVID-19   108

A Death in Winter   111

Notes   127
Acknowledgements   133

The Silver Garden

Blackout

10 p.m.

A keen torch beam
leads me up the steps,
left hand on the brass rail

as I recall the uniformed
usherettes of long ago
guiding latecomers to plump seats

then conjure Edward Hopper's
bored usherette, her spun-gold hair
a starlet's as she waits, spotlit

but out of sight, stood back from
the great smoky beam, the spell of
dream and desire it casts.

Now, two candles lit,
I lie facing the wide window,
my gaze travelling the moon-hazed sky,

its frozen waterfall of stars.
Only hours-old, a memory unfolds:
on a small screen, Iguazu Falls —

the monumental singing whiteness
of a river hurtling to meet itself
then brokenly ride the abyss.

In close-up, the Devil's Throat,
the misted gloom of its cliff-face
home to great dusky swifts,

their dark-adapted eyes agleam
as they fly out through splintered light
to hunt, fly back to perch

in slick, vertical squadrons
or zoom to clefts and ledges where,
on nests of moss, they feed their young.

2 a.m.

You can feel so
innocent, outside
in the cold dark.

Above a street lamp's
pale void, the full moon
magisterial, even as

the rim of its corona
billows, swept by
winds out of time —

an eye of light,
diamond-centred, ghosted by
the breath of an earthling.

Over my bare feet
shadows from the silver garden.
No bird voices.

6 a.m.

Though my desire for light
has passed, I step out
to accept the new day,

its comfort, reassurance.
The sunrise moon is
a worn-through version of

its night self,
the craters and seas
that cradled luminance

now a polite grey.
My blackbird's song —
Schubert, essentially,

with something of
the minimal surprise of
Satie — is laced with

rogue notes that hover,
unguessable,
then pivot towards

a new efflorescence,
touched by lyric joy
yet holding so much silence.

Unearthly

You've been up there yourself
looking down past a silver wing

at the shadows clouds cast
upon each other,

and those that travel oceans,
glitteringly dark as the great shoals.

Some slide over mountain islands —
erased in a breath, restored in a breath —

then nested cliffs, wheat fields, valleys:
even when at rest, in transit.

And, as on this beach now,
there are darknesses

sent from ethereal white
that can eclipse a summer's day,

turn our bones wintery —
until seabirds in flight

trawl glimmering wraiths
across the waters

while, with a gannet-dive,
Icarus falls into his own shadow.

When the sun itself sinks,
bloody and burnished,

archipelagos of cloud
send out thousand-mile shadows

cutting through that cold radiance,
probing the void.

Offstage the moon, in white-face, waits.
Waves harvest grey spume

above an inner twilight
thronged with opal-eyed bodies,

lanterns that breathe,
self-healing stars.

At last, upon the ocean
a shaft of moonlight

lustrous and bold,
lapped by blackness.

The wind, shadow-soft,
grows cooler, warmer.

Autumn Begins

As if the moon were my creature
I gaze and gaze —
pen and notebook in hand,
out in the last summer night.
But who is looking at whom?

I stand, light-shadowed
by the windows to my living room,
canny and intent,
at ease with the vision
of just the naked eye.

Aware, by now, I can never
in any true way, know what I see,
I look with fixity at utter
changeableness,
an intimate remoteness —

this sky-borne companion
that sways salt tides, the tides of
blood and mind, and has sown thoughts
too, of how the stars
impinge on us, writing our lifelines.

Clouds arise, drive westward —
the moon map with its inverse
Africa, its inverse Europe,
darkening until lost altogether
in a temporary new moon.

Then, through veils and vagaries,
through ragged gulfs, a gleaming
as of light-ensorcelled water:
within those shifting depths
a cabochon.

Continents re-appear,
becoming crystal quarries
as a total numb radiance
covers half the whole:
a glamour and grammar of influence,

a brooch pinned to the dreaming mind,
its chalcedony shine caught in
the self-renewing eyes of newts,
their bodies glistening like silver lures
under the power of the full moon.

'A History of the Lotus'

For months, alluringly,
the title floated in my mind,
yet I held back —
the research, without horizon
and the lotus itself, ineffable:

each gold-centred bloom
an icon of sacred wholeness;
trillions of them gracing lakes,
waterways, across millennia.

At last, a hasty first draft in hand,
I sat in the Gardens by the lotus pond,
there to drink coffee with a friend
while scoping each other's poems
for flaws, for modest bounties.

When its moment came, the page
curled into a scroll then was unfurled
by the waspish wind, borne aloft
and delivered like a letter into
a glimmer between lotus leaves.

The sun sparkled. The poem,
unretrievable, slanted skywards for now
amid chalices of white glass
tinctured with the pinks of amaranth, coral

and, movingly, the skin of that young raven,
glimpsed beneath wind-parted plumage
as it stepped over the lawn, hesitant,
its eyes in thrall to the newness of all life.

In the hazy, aromatic air
the lotus flowers, loftily poised
above their leaves, became
for a paused second,

    an array of lamps
    within a library
    where a florilegium
    lay open to reveal

    a lotus – itself a book
    composed of sculpted pages;
    a flawless crucible,
    alive with light.

Time then flowed forward
as I contemplated
the random poetry of drops,
fine as perfume spray,
upon those veined, succulent pages,

some capturing the shine of other drops
and even that ultimate glint
on its own blue page,
the sky of this day.

Late Spring Gardens

Rain falls on the Botanic Gardens,
its commonwealth of leaves —
almost unseen
but with force enough to be heard.

Many sounds, one sound.

On the Japanese Barberry,
its trunk half-eaten by ticks,
the bone of heartwood exposed,
ant trails ascend through

a long papery wound.

High up, in wreaths around
the boughs, yellow flowers
like pollen magnified,
and wreathing around them,

the bees, creating

as they work, a bee-voice,
a sonorous descant on the rain.
An atmosphere of harvest,
of nurturance, of damage,

carried on the air I breathe.

Later, at home, Bach will be waiting,
and other composers of silence,
of the movements of the soul,
small or epochal,

that would be traced, re-enacted

in closed rooms over centuries,
and sometimes in the scented
rooms of spring from where,
sometimes, bees could be heard

and faint, solacing rain.

In my own garden
the semibreves on the climbing rose
will harbour daylight, still;
the bees, soon to go home

or fall asleep in flowers.

Drifting out through the screen door
a cello suite will weave itself
around the leaves, the washed-pink
roses, the sturdy trunks,

each step I take a springboard

towards night, towards a new season
of lightning-seeded blazes
planted in ancient forests,
of ever more life in flight

as we approach the summer years.

Hold to the days of grace,
enter their brimming, humming air.
Amid rumours of flame
wait at midnight windows for

cool winds from Antarctica.

Cloud Life

There is something about
clouds seen through trees
newly in leaf — delicate
framings of transience

against a blue overworld,
with spy holes, cameos,
gem-flares among the unfurled.
Cached vistas disclose

the grandeur of becoming,
the triumph of the nebulous;
cycles of ravaging and healing,
of eclipse, efflorescence.

Each day I welcome, now,
whatever light is on offer,
the clouds a parable of how
darkness, radiance, may defer

to each other, even embrace,
even cohabit, then sheer apart
haunted by absence — faces,
eye-shapes, half-erased hearts

glimpsed in rustling windows —
until a full sky washes down,
leaving a glass shadow,
zenith-high: dusk at noon.

Introit

First light
of spring's first day.

On the sliding glass doors
of my blue house

colours garnered, it seems,
from endless orchards

of pomegranates,
tangerines.

The wind blows as if it means to be
felt, to be heard,

veers every which way,
all edge, all flow,

riddles and riffles
the winter-honed leaves.

What messages are hidden
in the balm of this wild wind

that might deliver us
from ourselves, and to ourselves

in times such as these —
so much of Earth's life

at the mercy of drought, fire, ice-melt,
of plagues, ancient or new;

in times such as these
when it can seem

we don't know who
we are, or where we are going.

Back in the present moment,
here,

the first yield ever of limes,
the lemon tree speaking, too,

and on the ageing apricot tree
one blossom.

A blackbird I know
lands on the back fence,

the curled plume in her beak
irradiated —

its glory a momentary
fact about the world —

then lifts into the leafy
deeps, nest bound.

After Rain

Early, overcast —
a sky of tattered winding-sheets.
Almost beyond sight, a silver eye
hints at another kind of day

but this is the light we have now,
within each drop
ornamenting the leaves,
a subdued glow.

On the jade plant,
droplets set close as seed pearls,
one leaf a glazed plateau;
among its splay of boughs,

two crystal planets —
one, aquiver, the other, still —
held by an infrastructure
my eyes at last perceive.

The rinsed air, tabula rasa,
is being written on by
tinctures of green, by lures
famous among bees, butterflies.

Filaments afloat on
a half-breeze waver,
stretch towards stillness
as if trying to thread needles.

A blackbird whisks through
a maze of twigs to her nest
inside the blue potato bush —
a mandala of leaves, mauve flowers.

From the nestlings, about to receive
a beak-hoard of worms,
a loud twittering throb —
even the voice of hunger, musical.

One day soon I'll see them —
twin chicks with stubby wings,
stout-breasted bodies,
eyes filled with black brightness.

Set trembling by my breath,
the jade tree's temporary planets
sparkle, grow calm, gleam wisely,
holding in trust the sky, the day.

Blackbird

I hate weeding
but decided that's what she wanted me to do —
so I'd leave holes in softened earth
for her to forage in.

Sure enough, she tracked me
across the vegetable patch,
her beak digging and plunging
with inquisitorial flair.

All day, brisk journeys between
front garden nest and the back garden.
Once, a winged thud that left
an insignia of oil on plate glass.

And sometimes, en route, she'll sing
atop the garden fence — mutedly,
with wriggling worms in her beak,
while, unmistakably, looking in at me.

This evening, the radio on,
she listened with lively interest
to an archived piano roll —
Gershwin's *Love walked in*

as played, inimitably,
by Percy Grainger — then, with full beak,
added her own version.
'Though not a word was spoken'

there was long eye contact
through the open window
until I thought,
Where am I going with this?

Still, if I can be some kind of
silent partner in her quest
to feed this second brood,
I'll do it.

Two from the first brood
I'd seen near the fence
amid round splotches of white,
dumbfounded but dauntless,

awaiting her next delivery,
their wings little hinges
able to lift them a few feet.
They lasted a day.

A currawong had been hanging around.
In my naivety
I'd paid it no mind
and only later, drew conclusions.

Meanwhile, along with the daily
yanking out of roots to expose
emporiums of worms,
I'm sure she'd like me to be

a guardian, too,
though what can I do – beyond,
on occasion, the shooing off
of killer birds and cats?

But she is a guardian to me,
a heartener-in-chief.
She'll keep at her tireless work
until pod-eyes open, and those wings,

bony and bare, become convincing –
while, at each return,
ever-strengthening throats
herald the glory of her coming.

Garden Walk, Daybreak

In smoked-glass light
a test of wakefulness:

poised, at face level,
above the shrub-edged path

a Golden Orb-weaver,
round-bodied on its wheel.

I stop, inches away,
break threads, over one branch

drape the web with spider –
both gone, minutes later.

Back and forth between
a garden gate besotted with

arcs of pink roses
and the front gate, its space for

the unlatching hand
an oculus – from one angle,

deeps of prescient grey,
moon-centred.

Today's first sky arrives –
newly invented colours

evoking, for a start,
fire and jewels,

sundry rose shades,
the orange of calendula

but, as always,
beyond metaphor, or naming.

At last, the poignancy of
the whole garden

with its lone bird, leaf-shaped,
high in a stripped tree.

Pure silence, then a soundless
absence of silence.

Now the delicate, jubilant voice
of next door's toddler.

I stand on rocks by the path
to glimpse, over the fence of

this hilltop house, the bay,
its far frontier of mist

meeting uncertainly
a sky already storied by

cloud journeys, light effects
from the risen sun.

Each human day
a crucible with hairline crack,

its beauty
beyond knowing.

The Unquiet Garden

A storm-wrenched tree
clothed in electric gold
divides the garden.

Quick dark presences
hop lustily around it,
stalk through undergrowth

like shadow thoughts
glimpsed at the mind's edge
as I sit within the tensile

silence of this room,
my gaze opening to admit
surprise, elusiveness.

When John, my Irish friend,
comes to tend the garden,
there's one walks by so close

he imagines, half-believes,
it might somehow carry
the spirit of his dead brother.

'A lovely thought,' I say.
'He must be very old,'
says John, now in his nineties.

And we watch our shared
familiar, his eyes unwarily
taking account of us as he skirts

the space where we work.
On the garden fence
outside my kitchen, he seems

to be looking in at me
while seeming not to (he knows
I know he knows I'm here).

Up on the apricot tree
another kind of looking, then
silver palaces in the air:

a living silhouette,
not knowing how many songs
are yet to be sung,

his feet planted among
the unleashed delicacy of
day-old blossom.

Zen Morning

I pace the driveway, up and down,
breathing myself into the day.
On high-summer blue, a halved
moon that was, a week ago,
a blue moon, an eclipsing blood moon,
held in millions of eyes.

Along a stave of powerlines,
convocations of magpies, starlings;
a lone honeyeater balances,
is still, looks near and far,
manifests, moment by moment,
its intelligence, its freedom.

Near the gate, a white stone horse
the size of a year-old child.
Lifelike and mythic, it lies
folded around its own stillness, earthed:
mustard-gold moss over its back,
an imprimatur of birdlime.

My jade tree, all the leaves and flowers
of this garden − butterfly bush,
jasmine, *myrtus luma* − flourish,
each presence nurtures further life.
I flow with the blessed air.
The whole garden breathes through me.

For a silent hour here I stay,
claimed by this peace, this fragrance.
With dauntless power, with anchoring cries,
black cockatoos, at great height,
head toward cypresses by the bay,
where they'll gather, feed.

The White Cockatoos

At a sunlit window I stand,
marked by flicking shadows
as hundreds fly over, headed towards
their feeding grounds — so low today
the sense of an enfolding, as if
they would take this house with them.

A wind-tossed babel fills the mind:
voicings of exultant power
spliced with plain conversation
and the bonding calls of families,
of young peer groups,
each with their own sound-code.

Sometimes, witnessing these journeys,
I hear cries, harsh and aggrieved,
as yet more trees are felled for houses,
perhaps even a note of panic —
as if they sensed, somewhere beyond,
a devouring emptiness.

Once, among trees by the bay,
I heard a susurrus, as of
a wind machine adding atmosphere
to an old opera, an eerie frisson,
saw, felt, their passage close above,
a speeding white sky.

Later, far off, homeward-bound cockatoos
roving between each other
as they travelled beneath clouds
gravid with night-blue dust,
their plumage, enamel-sleek, aglitter,
parrying the sun's last gift.

Visitations

White butterflies
glancing off a breeze

along cliff-top grasses —
a frieze of lacemakers

intricately at work
beneath the bay's

array of scintilla:
stars of an instant only,

each rhapsodic flare
a bloom in a garden

swept by the clouds'
unsettled silver.

I walk on past inklings
that pulse fervidly,

with pauses to sip,
across the daisied fields.

Flat on the path
a wanderer butterfly

lets its design speak
from absolute stillness,

the eyeless wings
a luminance

of honeyed orange
with black veins looped

to conjure petals,
the whole flower.

Up and gone before
I can breathe,

now suddenly back,
its kiss on my wrist.

Summer Poem

Slight tilts of the head, of the gaze,
reveal, high up between
leaf-laden branches,

fugitive glintings along
a taut line — syllables of light
linking, breaking apart, in flow.

Or, you can wait in stillness
until incidental sways of air
do the work for you.

Meanwhile, close by,
shrubs, even the clipped hedge,
harbour threads that become

orbed veils, cramped, fallen
wings, would-be holograms
ready to shine,

needing only an angle of sun,
a release of this breath-held air —
which will come, will come.

Poetry, too, is essence
payed out, played out, into form,
an existential blueprint

that builds from a silken line
with a feeling of light along it,
of air around it,

to become an articulated
shape, a simple
luminosity

able to shift the gaze,
be shifted by it —
so creating, even on

the difficult days,
the days of foreclosure,
an atmosphere of belief,

of presence at peace with
failure, loss,
of beauty in love with truth.

At the Solstice

Days of the dragonfly, the cicada.
Yet even in this mild zone
an upheaval of plenitude –
a month's rain in one day
bathing the deepest roots.

I lie meditating, break off
to scribble notes for a poem,
this poem, resume slow breathing.
In the room somewhere
a page falls to the floor.

At just this moment I recall
the decades of melancholia, despair –
small change in the scheme of things.
Another lifetime would be needed
to voice my thankfulness for the rest.

To the bay! – with sightings en route
of a blackbird whose closed beak
holds a bead of sunlight,
a ribboned skyburst of mynahs,
each white wing patch, irradiated.

The cliffs with their wild gardens.
Down the slopes, agapanthus,
silver-green succulents;
by the path, clumps of tea tree,
gorse, sea-heath, saltbush.

Within the bars of a leafy cage
a superb fairy-wren takes pause
as if to contemplate his options —
all simple, all blue.
Swallows orbit, never mistaken,

while high above, the inspirational
dignity of ibis, with one shared goal,
tending the spaces between —
a calibrated closeness amid
knots, velleities of air.

The sky, the sea — two kinds of
transparency, almost seamless.
Later, dusk winds will draw
darkness up through the waters,
scrawls of ink on glistening pages.

Midsummer

At Clifton Springs

The Infinite a sudden Guest
Has been assumed to be —
But how can that stupendous come
Which never went away?
  — Emily Dickinson

Stumps from an old pier
track out into the bay —
resting posts for terns,
pelicans, cormorants.

Through the gleaming miles
dark with seabed rock,
a channel of lucid green
winds like a river.

I stand on the cliff-top,
breath slowed. The salt wind
leans companionably
on bare shoulders.

Along the shore,
children and dogs at play,
tranced walkers beside
shadowless waves —

hostages, all, to the day's
hymn of becoming.
I move on past shining
grasses, sea box, *correa alba*.

High over the bay
a kelp gull glides in a long arc,
a yielding, shaping gesture,
then slows into flight.

Thin clouds under the blue
cast a snow field onto
the waters, boats carving
furrows of light through it.

Beyond the drama of tides,
the You Yangs rise from
Wadawurrung Country –
in whose clasp this bay lies.

The sun offers its strength,
pitch-perfect on the skin.
This moment is all moments.
Accept, be blest.

Late Summer Sea

After weeks of dangerous heat
the summer may yet, if I allow it,
yield a flowering of
hope and fulfilment —

perhaps now, at last, as I stand
thigh-deep in the sea,
nerving up for immersion —
the low peaks puddled with cold light,

the horizon's arced thread
the sky's only boundary as it lifts
through versions of blueness
to utter, incontrovertible blue.

At one with so much light,
with air's infinite presence,
I imagine myself a glow worm,
tiny and compact inside

summer's transparent vessel
then assume another life form
to flow beneath a cresting sky,
realms of sun-inflected green:

    the plunge, the thrilling shock,
    each dive's slow curve broken by
    heave, onrush — the sea's will
    having it out with mine —

till the emergence, buoyed, breathless,
to resume the weight of my body,
let it carry that stored sunfire,
that glorious clasp of chill, home.

Anniversary Visit

At Barwon Heads

I've driven across the peninsula
with a clasp of lavender, daphne, red salvia
to throw onto the river —
a fling of gratitude, as it were,
for the years spent here with my mother
and now, the book written in her memory.

The flowered stems are on the waves,
slate and moonstone, heading seaward.
From the jetty I glimpse a diamond-shape
riding, massaging the current,
its wings undulating
like some wonderful form of thought.

The manta sweeps under the jetty,
vanishes — so calling to mind
a summer long ago: a basking presence
that sped off, confounding my gaze,
as my feet touched lapping water.
I waded in, crouched where it had hovered.

Today's visit of a living darkness
revealing then recusing itself
is pure gift, I take no lesson from it —
this miraculous shadow flowing where
need and curiosity take it, sea-dancing
under the cold, lapidary waves.

Bowers

Forever — is composed of Nows —
   — Emily Dickinson

Day after wintery day,
fatigue, a lifelong bane,
present in every cell —
infinitesimal phials of it
slowly leaking out.

The Solstice draws near.
I begin to imagine
lying here, ready or not,
wrapped in the sky-cloak
I have woven from my life.

Out in the garden, no wind,
the tree of unknown name
still, but for a low branch
bobbing, quivering —
a bower claimed, I see now,

by that honeyeater, busy
among, above and under
the perfumed white flowers,
with no need to imagine
a sky-cloak, or dying.

In thrall to questions
too imponderable to ask,
I turn to Emily Dickinson,
standing, beyond aloneness,
on her 'Blue Peninsula',

open her riddling-
and-ravishing volume,
a thought-world of poems
written on the wing –
so light, so quick, so deep.

After a timeless time,
some back and forth,
an understanding is reached –
Eternity
(which contains all death, all life)

might be imaged, perhaps,
for this moment at least,
as a tree with numberless
silver-leaved boughs,
each hosting white flowers

to be sipped and supped from
by honeyeaters who,
using intricate footwork
with adjunct wing-power,
reach to delve and drink

while, their feet hardly worth
naming as such,
the hummingbirds,
embodied yet ethereal,
their wings angelic motors,

the most sky-like wings of all,
hover, tuned perfectly to
time and timelessness,
taking their nourishment
from the nectared tree.

Weaving in and out of
its trove of bowers,
these spirit birds celebrate
a wedding of grace and nature,
of elegance and need,

their wings creating
delicate winds which fan
each flower's perfume out into
infinite darkness,
infinite light.

In Winter Light

Below the far rim of the bay,
like a white shadow
cast by the mountains,
that band of brilliance
still as a lagoon.

Across silent grey
a stream of sun glitter
pulses toward me, travels
in concert with my steps until
the path enters the trees.

I stop at last, turning
to find myself inside
the containing shadow
of a eucalypt,
slim-branched, silky grey,

and walk through rooms
shaped like pieces of stained glass,
the floors, grass or stony earth,
that curving wreath-edge
darkly consoling.

Back home, I stand amidst
skeins of shadow lines
cast by my own trees,
a thread of blanched silver
along each bough. It's noon,

daybreak's sky of snow
now a sea of glaciers
too bright to look at. *A lifetime,*
running after the light…
My hand rests on a branch.

In Silent Rooms

Glass Flowers

On Dena Kahan's *Glass Garden* paintings

1

Alchemical vessels
imbued with rumours of colour —
a pearly acorn-brown,
tinctures of amber, buff-white:

the Trickster, light,
mixing it up, sheathing
each sculpted bloom
in the glow of other objects;

even the innermost
whorl, the nectary,
shot through with
moody brilliance.

2

It cannot do harm:
fill them with pure water
then from a glass straw

sip the essence of these
flawless ghost-flowers
given body by breath.

As each goblet empties,
a volatile perfection
is restored,

ethereal dabs
and baubles gleam,
unrefracted.

3

Or, ply a window box of them
with graduated heights of water,
take a silver baton
and start the music:

a choir of glass flowers
voicing songs of
rootless transcendence.

Wind-chimes under the ocean.

4

A time-lapse camera
would show these flowers
in violent metamorphosis:

tarry with darkness,
slicked by ivory moonlight,
dawn's lava-red —

always in transit, becoming;
always, even when knifed by sun glare,
sealed, silent.

5

Seeded in fire,
amaryllis, iris, orchid —

sleek-skinned botanical studies

as vacant as living flowers are lush,
as brittle as living flowers are yielding.

Hothouse simulacra,
they lean towards windows

blank with rain,
bronze with day's last embers.

6

In art's parallel universe
a flower can tilt up from a bench top,

grow from it —
eerily resplendent;

return the beholder's gaze
with silken candour.

7

Each unfurled bloom,
each bud, enshrines
a Janus-truth:

sepals, curlicues
of varnished air
wear and witness

flux, never-ending
illusion, stay in thrall
to stillness.

And the long stems
seemingly
lit from within —

they too know the touch
of sky-shine, the quixotic
life of clouds.

Let's call it
the provisional sublime.

8

The exquisite can be so cold.

But these sprays,
their silvery leaf-wings poised,

express a sunflower-yearning:
rearing up, opening out,

as is the way of plant life
and of human desire —

so outright,
heroic, in a way

and, in the end, unanswerable.

   9

Stillness invites space.

Museums are built around
such dreamed embodiments

of the life we find here,
of the life that finds us.

The glass flowers
offer themselves —

enigmatic
constructions of hope.

They have survived
a seismic century.

Petals shaped like tongues,
like flames, radiate from

chambers of translucent
nothingness.

The Yellow Room

It will forever be
October, twenty-eighteen,
in this corner of my house

where a hung calendar displays
The Chinese Screen by Margaret Olley,
set in her heaven-on-earth living room

with a doorway into a further room,
blue-walled — below its window,
steeped in silver, a figured jar.

In the near room, an offstage
window offers its broad
slant on things, emblazons

the ochre-and-gold at the screen's centre,
falls on a flank of yellow wall,
the daybed's vined, flowered coverlet

and, with only one cup, the coffee set,
its grooved whiteness
a provocation to shadow.

How many times, over the many years
was this yellow room
conjured through paint, to become

witness and archive of
a life lived in art,
and of the life of art itself:

here, the headlong anarchic whirl
of Matisse's round of dancers
counterbalancing

the inturned calm, the storied
mystery, of the Chinese screen
with its pavilions, its robed figures

and a beyond of islands
on a blackly shining sea.
When evening comes

the room, no longer captive
to sliding shadows,
knows the solace of music –

its geometric airiness,
its aqueous flare-and-shimmer.
Then, humdrum pleasures,

and the sustenance, ease,
that enable the long moment of
a whole life.

Soon enough, sleep's erasures,
the neon shock of dreams,
whatever kind of rest is given

until first light reaches in
to place its touch upon
the things darkness saves for us.

Face

It's all a learning curve, hopefully going up.
 – Margaret Olley

In Silent Rooms

Always, in her mirror portraits,
an awareness of self as illusion,
even as her brush dips,

busy as a honeyeater,
into coils and surges of
colour incarnate.

At times, therefore,
what might be
a self-effacing smile, or

a would-be smile,
accompanied by a look
that might be wistful,

relaxed in kindness, or curious.
Only Margaret could have said.
Perhaps.

She made her accord with
illusion – with the evanescence,
as with the solidity

of presence,
was sustained in this by
the unbreathing stillness of

the flowers and fruits,
the postcard icons,
so often arrayed beneath

her unsurprised face
surprising itself in mirrors
atop dresser or mantlepiece.

Portrait in the mirror

In this first, famed portrait
her youthful face hovers
like a risen moon

above a tableau of conch shells,
everlasting daisies,
ripe fruits that give a loading of

cinnabar to the work;
then the miniatures,
one a Renaissance portrait,

in profile to her own full face,
of a woman, high-browed, wearing
as she does, a pearl necklace.

The wall behind has a sea-glimmer,
its celadon green swept by
ebbs and flows of radiance.

Art-making is already
the gist of her life, a workaday
pleasure, a practical dream,

an initiation into the secret
byways of colour, its alchemical
nectars preserving earth-gifts,

small galleries of splendour,
chaste vases in thrall to
the bravura of cut flowers.

Dressing table (self portrait)

The tilt of an old-fashioned
mirror-on-a-stand finds her.
On that carved platform,

artefacts of contemplation,
the glass vessels of beauty,
become a luminous threshold

guarding her bereaved self.
Her dream gaze looks inward
and, at a sideways angle, outward.

The iris of her left eye
holds a catchlight
like a misshapen tear.

Set against the mirror,
a mask-image, lids steeply closed
in meditation, or death,

takes shape from arctic blue,
teal, and the chrome green
so loved by the artist.

Those same colours live in
the wallpaper's summer leaves,
winding across backlit lapis —

sumptuous, yet end-of-day sombre:
    the blue of mortality,
    the blue of immortality.

Daylight fans in, leaving
half her face in shadow while
enfolding these chosen things,

precious or plain,
which speak the inspiration of
Chardin, of Morandi —

who laboured freely, exactly,
devotees of the numinous lure
of the inanimate.

Her musing self,
eye to eye with its double,
drinks, sip by sip,

a draught of truth
as the room, and the world,
fade, bloom.

Coda

So, Margaret Olley worked on,
worked on and on,
hoping that her painting life

    set amidst a tumult of
    stacked, half-finished canvases,
    brushes awry in pots,

    palettes of blood and pollen and jet —
    with everywhere, and always,
    flowers —

would endure until
her last day.
As it did.

The Black Cockatoos

On photographs by Leila Jeffreys

As if, surely,
they recognise
her joy in them,

wear it welcomingly
on their own gaze,
they create, with her,

a mutual stillness.
Then her finger
moves.

Some carry stories,
cryptically
hidden but present,

of dispossession
from empires of
fruited green,

from wide-armed
darknesses hung with
seed cones — brought down,

brought down fast,
to create miles of
moneyed space.

Let each gaze speak.
Where there is gentleness
let gentleness speak,

or feisty idiosyncrasy
or curiosity
or spry charm.

Even as the studio light
plants a white moon
in each brown eye

these cockatoos reveal
their essential selves,
enter, inhabit

an out-of-time poise,
everything stripped back
to wonder.

Have so many losses
in our overlapping worlds
wrought a new intimacy —

with each bird offering
freely, a knowledge
beyond our own?

Every portrait,
sideways on, holds
one mandalic eye —

a gleaming
pool of awareness,
lucid and deep.

The Red-tailed females
have particles of gold leaf
strewn across

breast, face feathers,
their counterpart flaunts
a mirage-tincture

of turquoise, ready to
point up or subvert
his varnished black.

On the Yellow-tailed,
near-gold rims
scalloped body feathers,

forms traceries
on the recumbent wings,
glows from cheek-puffs.

Their given names are
Nora, Melba, Rosie
and Pete, his crest and head

a furore of feathers,
that centred eye
all the more steadfast.

Akalla is the Glossy black,
recently ill,
still gathered into herself

but wearing a humble pride,
her measure of gold
dusted around her throat.

And what of Kirra,
a Carnaby's black cockatoo,
the species most under threat:

deliciously, delicately
beautiful in plumage
and in her mien,

crossing a line somewhere
to share in our nature,
allow us to share in hers.

From the photographer
with her spellbound patience
no smile-provoking jokes —

though with cockatoos
themselves, the risk
is always there.

The miniature studio,
world within world,
a bough its only prop,

is an open cage of light,
this imaging
an act of tending.

If you wait long enough
you can begin to see,
even to feel

the spirit of these birds,
their verve, resilience,
their wild, raw joy,

to long for their voices,
raucous and vivacious,
as with silent composure

they look toward us, through
the eyes of their photographer —
memorialist, celebrant, lover.

Portraiture

On the photography of Eugène Atget

Despite their documentary intent, Atget's images
seem to want to be placed in a story.
  — Nicholas Mirzoeff

Au Tambour, 63 quai de la Tournelle (5e arr.), 1908

On the pavement, a man at his work.
A waiter with chevron moustache
peers out, gravely curious;
a second face, woolly with whiskers —
that of the restaurateur, perhaps —
seems chuffed, if somewhat bemused.

They stand at the windowed door
before their workday begins with
the first order taken, the first coffee poured.
The large room behind them, empty.
What they can see — far trees,
a raft of dazzle on the Seine —

is reflected in the door's glass —
the photographer, too,
in a trick shot whereby
his dark-coated body, *sans tête*,
holds up the head of the older man.
Beneath its black shroud, the camera.

Boutique empire, rue du Faubourg-Saint-Honoré, 1902

But here he is, head intact, sideways
to his camera, seemingly within
the showroom of Boutique Empire
where an elegant, airy table
blocks out his lower body.
His mind is in his poised hands.

This is concentration, this is stillness
as the great glass facade
is miniaturised onto a glass plate,
so grafting the photographer —
witness and interloper — into this space
of moneyed taste, material grandeur.

The Square

A self-secluded man, he made no claims
for himself, or for the body of work
that imaged dwellings, shops,
whole streetscapes of Old Paris —
many, soon to vanish. And there were
portraits of organ grinders, knife-grinders,

sellers of lampshades, brollies:
as Paris was remade, they'd vanish, too.
Each stands in an unseen spotlight
while, in his singular, patient way
but with Balzacian belief,
Atget photographs them, forever.

And he archived the shanty-towns —
beside a rise of sheds, cabins,
the rag-and-bone men, their solemn-eyed
children looking back at us.
All this with his massive, antiquated
camera, hefted around Paris for decades.

The Surrealists, in their universe of
found objects, discovered him,
prized his pavement displays of
spat boots, cauliflowers, corsets, dolls,
his storefront windows with clouds in flux
above the staring eyes of mannequins.

What he loved most was
early morning light, ashen, sheer,
when the actor, and the painter
he had been, could apprise
then set forth a *mise-en-scène*,
whether spectral and decaying,

with playbills lifting from alley walls,
or exquisitely bare, resonant with
the absence of life and lives.
He sets up in a Square, like a silent room:
Eugène Atget, elegist, working on
as if nothing can be truly lost.

At Niagara Galleries

1

I stand before the lethal churn
of three-storey breakers
about to inundate these rooms

and in the shadow-path of
wind-sloped cypresses,
gothic above a foreshore.

Next, a corner of coast
with defunct boathouses,
a terminal open to sky.

A ship's hulk eats the horizon,
another looms, dock-side, beyond
an edifice of lost purpose.

I walk on, stop to catch
the running man, fleeing from
cataclysmic tides

then, nightmare followed by
waking dream, the watcher
on a pier, and the brown dog

sitting among the dunes —
each utterly alone, gazing seaward...
All these, as summoned by Rick Amor,

an adept of the cutting power
of light, its livid-pink diffusions
pre-storm, its dystopian glare

blanketing innocent seaside towns,
its liminal, night-in-day gleam
keeping darkness at bay.

2

The buffed boards resound.
I enter the spectral lanes
and cul-de-sacs of a city at dusk

then, 'the outlying districts' where,
aloft on a pillar, an unfinished span
stubs the air; beside it, a bridge

making ready to forget itself.
Beneath a swerve of concrete,
a car bursts into flames.

Two figures pass an eye of river,
moon-engulfed; the silhouette of
an idol lifts above ramparts.

3

Meanwhile, close but far away,
in a museum's catacomb rooms,
in its cavernous halls,

the atavistic aura of vanished
life – our antecedents caged
inside vitrine reflections;

the gigantism of
demigods sculpted from shadows;
and the skull of a mammoth

eased from locked earth,
dusted off, set on black rods, spotlit:
ruin lust taken to a further level.

Cold around your shoulders
the architecture of power, framing
these artefacts of absence,

even the air itself,
the drab light, vestigial,
courting extinction.

4

The Room (Memory)

i

In this vacant, tenebrous room
so many versions of light.
It leaks in, wisps in

from around the closed blind:
a triptych of shadows,
a haloed portal.

The luminance spreads, claims
small territories on floor and ceiling,
imbues the wardrobe's mirror

with silken white smoke,
reaches the dressing gown
hung on the open door, handles it.

Everything else, save
the wardrobe's glimpsed darkness,
is a calibration of grey,

the limbo colour –
while yet, as in old snapshots
trapped between black and white,

a seeming guarantor of
clear intent, a curator of
dream-memories, rich or searing.

ii

We are made up – so we know
now – mostly of space,
atomic space.

And we hunger for space –
for infinite space, yes,
but also for space, confined,

intimate, as within
the rooms of our lives
surrounding us with

solid rectangles,
with emptiness, cubed,
with indelible atmospheres.

At times they draw us
back, these rooms, toward the silences
of inner space, toward

the pulse, finite and faithful,
of soul and heart, letting us overhear
their answer to dread.

The Postcard

Reflections on Rick Amor's
Self-portrait with postcard of Greco Roman bust

1

Brought to material life
in calm, anchoring rooms,
a half century of self-portraits —

one placed in each exhibition,
decade after decade,
a kind of signature.

This portrait, never seen by me,
has been translated onto lush paper,
even its darker tints, satined.

In my many-windowed room
I angle the page to catch the sun.
Now I can see for sure

those eyes harbour no inkling
of light, though the right eye,
focused on itself and on the viewer,

looks intently out. The left eye,
seemingly recused, more opaque,
has played its full part.

Meanwhile, the face, the upper body
attest a chosen stillness.
Whatever pain or struggle,

stoicism or hope, may be held
within that body, the artist's bearing
maintains an austere dignity –

an inner stance expressive of
self-command, hungering purpose,
the power and privilege of the gift.

The white shirt, mostly anything but
white, is a ritual garment
affording its own study of

the metaphysics of light-and-darkness
as grey tones slide downward,
the passages of white, near-diaphanous.

The outstretched right arm,
that hand, surely at rest upon a frame,
say agency, lay their claim.

　　2

Notes. Read in any order.

In this self-portrait
　　darkness is a servant of the whole
　　each stroke of white,
　　bounty, and blessing

the unseen palette
    is the servant of
    mortar and cloth, flesh and wood

the unseen mirror
    makes its fleeting claim on truth
    turns a living gaze into illusion

the uncanvased frame
    is a grid of nothingness,
        of potentiality,
    invokes the dharma of
        geometrical order

the wall on which it rests
    is a vibrant abstraction
        made from cloud particles,
        from traces of sunlight
        on nameless blue –
    or seems so, at this moment

the room's space
    is, as ever,
    an ambit of the soul,
    now fraught, now tranquil –
        'cliffs of fall',
        a haven of the human

the room's silence
    contains many silences
    but there are whispers of brushwork,
    paint tubes clunk down

the room's atmosphere
    breathes itself into
    the artist's mind, his lungs,
    out through his fingers

the presence created
    is the harvest of skill and sentience,
    grace, assiduous patience

the unseen window
    upper left, has determined
    the placing of the subject,
    the vehemence of the light
            touching his skull
    the temperature of brightness

the wristwatch
    is a *memento mori*

the canvased frame,
    this final work,
    is a fiction of imperishability

the post card
    is a muse,
    two millennia old:
        between the woman imaged,
            and the artist,
      a spiral of time —
    a chambered whorl,
        as in a nautilus shell,
            of makers, masters

3

And the whole litany of self-portraits?

a mirror-quest —
    mirage after mirage,
    each an earnest of
    full disclosure

a homage to time —
    many breaths in the making

inspiration as aspiration
    ('the craft so long to learn')

the alchemy of influence —
    in unknown rooms,
    paintings with a second signature

a primer without text —
    each new reveal of gold,
    each prescient shadow, a seed

a detective story —
    all clues in plain sight
    an investigation in train
    the mind with its catchlight

The Room

A raven, winter-hungry or curious,
checks out the front garden,
struts to the glass doors I sit behind
and, seeing me, my gaze,

jumps in fright, lifts to the fence —
instantly back on the qui vive:
at each head shift, cloud light
sliding on oiled ebony.

Inside this room with its wall-high
windows, its tree-veiled light,
a sequestered feel, the hearth's
glassed-in flames a winter muse.

On the walls, gold-framed pictures,
gifts of the artists or of friends...
Birds-of-paradise, as viewed by Ellis Rowan
on late-life journeys to New Guinea.

Margaret Stones, her realm the flora of
Tasmania, Louisiana, everywhere —
each self-composed plant a conundrum,
serenely out of time.

And here, life at three removes:
Dena Kahan's study for a painting of
flowers, fashioned in glass long ago
to teach, to invite wonder.

Flame-licked amber, pink, vermilion,
all with circlets of yellow –
Margaret Olley's poppies in a jar,
self-vanquishingly open.

Clarice Beckett, her richness
one of sparsity, offers a bay scene,
a red boat doubled in the gleam:
each colour so at home with light.

To complement its black-and-white,
Rick Amor's *Street at Night*
with solitary walker, faint moon,
hangs beside a photograph of

Monet, stood before a window wall,
its curtains, waterfalls of spring light;
on the left, a wall of paintings, his own –
days, months, years – edge to edge.

This will be winter's coldest day.
It's 8 a.m. A golden blade slides down
objects on a table: the carved
flamingo feeding her chick,

a salt lamp, a bronze Buddha
and, framed by chrysoprase-green,
three airborne medieval angels
playing their trumpets while –

the phenomenal world has its tropes, too —
their robes, irradiated for seconds only,
shimmer in the fire's fanned heat:
tiny ripples, as from eternity's ocean.

For the rest, a chaos of drafts and folders,
books on birds, poetry, art,
the laptop with its troves of images.
All, part of the room's biography, and mine.

The only living thing, a peace lily
in a battered copper pot, sweeps
upward, outward — its leaves,
lissomely curved, a silk-and-satin green.

No flowers yet; one nibbed shoot
soon to unfurl. Meanwhile, tall vistas
of branches, bare, budded or leaved,
a sky set to rain, or not rain, as it will.

Rooms by the Sea

On the painting by Edward Hopper

Maybe I am not very human. What I wanted to do
was to paint sunlight on the side of a house.
  — Edward Hopper

I

That further room, a tenth of the whole,
a mere column, with its tranche of light
slanting in across the life of things:
red chair and green carpet; a painting —
sun-glazed, its story untold; the bookcase
whose unseen books touch each other
or lie alone, ready to enter your thoughts,
for your thoughts to enter them.

That further room. It must have granted
ease and pleasure, the solace of dailiness.
In the painter's psyche, in the economy of
his life at the easel, master and captive,
the fact of this room, what it configured,
amounting to a tithe. Is that a fair guess?

II

The closer room is the main game
with its insert of radiance hingeing
wall and floor – an origami of sunlight
you could lean against, warm bare feet on.
The doorway holds, as in a tumbler, ocean
dauntingly at its work, a sky of mauve, cobalt.
The door, compact as a sentinel, waits.

So this is it: the archetypal real.
A room, stripped, complete.
                              A perilous openness.
Even the shadows, inscaped with light –
blue-quartz ghosting slate grey.
Under a short horizon, the sea's archaic
pulse and thrash, salt air billowing.
Breathe in, out; breathe in.

Lake with Moonlight

On John Atkinson Grimshaw's
Moonlight on the lake, Roundhay Park, Leeds

The surprise of the full moon
between blind and window frame —

a heliodor watch-face
on a band of night-wreathed cloud —

as I sit through the hour before dawn
regarding moonlight on water.

The furthest trees, a gauzy brown,
spill into the lake, become

a sunken cliff-face
raked with ochre, amber.

In the foreground, silhouette-sharp,
a gothic frame of trunks

with leafless twigs spiking in
to pincer the moon,

naked and mist-bound:
a beacon, a simulacrum.

There are two pathways.
Moonlight's unrolled silk,

white as baptismal robe,
bridal train, shroud,

a boat's wake, ever-transforming,
on the drift of stillness.

The other path, earthen,
ends at a picket gate —

a threshold to be breached,
so you step down,

squelch through mud and moonlight
beside the cold-fleshed lake,

hear, and see
the unheard, the unseen

as a myriad of creatures
shape their pathways —

dark within the darkness,
light inscribed on light —

moving under and through
the sky's composite of

luminous green, dust grey,
its illusory gravitas.

Then your eyes, your mind,
ask to be rested.

Within the painting, woodpeckers
and willow warblers sleep on

but here, the spruikers and poets
are already sprucing the air,

the real-time moon
has slipped from view.

The lit screen darkens,
the day breaks.

Flight to the Stars

On Tjungkara Ken's *Kungkarangkalpa tjukurpa*
(Seven Sisters dreaming), a self-portrait

I hold my father's story, I hold my mother's story… [it] doesn't come
out of paper or out of a book. It's coming out of the ground here.
…
My painting is a self-portrait through Kungkarangkalpa tjukurpa,
the Seven Sisters dreaming – a self-portrait of my country.
For Anangu, they are one and the same.
  – Tjungkara Ken

At the Archibald Portrait Prize, 2017

In the crowded gallery
the etiquette of a popular exhibition
rules – one person at a time

stepping in close to apprise
a detail, almost touch
the topography of texture

then moving back to join
the fluid knot of gazers,
view the picture whole.

Some paintings ask for
greater distance from their
elaboration of a vision,

a slower attentiveness to their
inscape of meaning –
none more so than this one,

without a human figure
or a face, though it is given as,
named as, self-portrait.

With its reverberant lines
marking ancient trails,
its waterholes ringed with

ochre, black, bronze,
with its earth, its ground of being,
deep-tinctured in red,

this painting offers an image of
heartland, place of belonging
millennia upon millennia.

And here too, constellated
in this earthscape,
are stars that embody

the story of seven sisters
who nightly fled from a pursuer
by leaping into the sky,

becoming a star cluster,
The Seven Sisters —
shining close above the horizon

then at each dawn, travelling
down and back again
to live the next new day

in the flow of eternity
and storied time,
on the sacred ground of Country.

In the crowded gallery, I hold back,
aware of the limits of
my own understanding

then step in close,
let this redness wash into me —
the red of the desert earth,

the red of suffering and shed blood,
the red of hope, regeneration.
Red.

Shimmer

Ms. G (Djotarra) Yunupingu is survived by a large family and a circle of friends across the world. In recognition of her international importance the family have consented to her name appearing in text, but requested that no image be shown, and that her first name not be uttered. Instead she can be referred to as Djotarra or Ms Yunupingu.
  — Jeremy Eccles

Yolŋu judge a bark painting in terms of the light and luminosity created by its cross-hatching. In art from East Arnhem Land a complex transformation process takes place, causing the bark surface to change from its natural dull tone to bir'yun, *or brilliant. The expression of luminosity through shimmer is the basis of Yolŋu aesthetics.*
  — Georges Petitjean

Nothing but Stars

Djotarra — mother, healer,
comforter of the dying,
cultural and community leader
and an artist on many fronts,
began her work as a painter
late in life, the starred sky
her one subject.

I've stood before a painting
where close-meshed stars
swirl across the contours of
a great sheet of bark,
rhythmed as if by
intricate flows of water,

and have felt, as a presence,
the unseen reaches of
her vision of the universe —
even while I stayed earthed,
gazing from this smallness,
my mind silenced by the mystery.

The sky unifies us,
so Djotarra believed.
We can all look at the stars,
whichever sky we're looking at.

And she said: *If we could see*
everything that exists in the night sky,
we would see nothing but stars.

A Ceiling in Paris

Djotarra was one of eight Indigenous Australian artists invited to create
works for the Musée du Quai Branly. A night sky with thousands of stars,
painted in white, black, and red and yellow ochres, covers a ceiling (which is
illuminated at night), on the second floor. At the opening ceremony in 2006,
she spoke of wishing to share her art and culture: 'This is my gift to you,
to the French people, and to the people of the world, this is my heart.'

Suppose yourself in Paris,
walking at night past
the Musée du Quai Branly.

Your gaze passes through its glass walls
to a ceiling that has become
a resplendent sky.

And in daylight you might see,
from inside the Museum,
the Eiffel Tower

needling up through
the ceiling's starry reflection
in the vertical glass.

Her first name, now unspoken,
carried this meaning:
'the star shining from the North'.

Once, when a child,
camping out with her family
on a cloudless night, she felt

a light moisture settling on her skin —
'Maybe it's the stars crying'
was her mother's thought.

Decades later, when Djotarra
painted the stars, some would have
at their centre, an eye.

Djotarra Dying

Her whole community
came to be with her
through the last days of her life,
camping in the hospital grounds,
the children running along
corridors, playing on the grass.

As she lay in a coma,
her sisters keening around her,
a recording of that same
sacred keening, the *milkarri*,
was played from a mobile phone
placed on her pillow:
the voice of Gaymala,
the sister who had died.
Djotarra, though unconscious,
joined her older sister in keening.

She had lived with the belief
that once gone from this life,
her spirit would take its place
among the stars, with her ancestors,
while also present with them
within the bodies of water of
her Country, North East Arnhem Land.

The stars, the dark, bright waters
shining inside each other.

Her Blessing

Among the boundless gifts
that are her legacy,
Djotarra left these words:
The truth lies in what every artist has to say;
there is healing for people when they see beauty.

Dancer

Reflections on *The inner stillness of Eileen Kramer*
by Andrew Lloyd Greensmith

I do feel that I'm full of this beauty of breath. Breath is life.
  – Eileen Kramer, 2017

    1

Sometimes, time
is against you, it is your enemy
and sometimes it is with you

    as you walk on, dance on
    through the wilds of your life –

as if time, also, has learnt
to breathe in deeply,
hold, accept,
breathe slowly out –

    relaxing into
    the pure moment of itself.

    2

What might someone,
now and always a dancer,
still teaching others

how to craft and shape
the spirit of dance,
look like, at the age of
one hundred and two?

I'm standing before
the portrait of a woman
with closed eyes,
her hands delicately cupping,
almost, her tilted head.

In her face, in her composure,
a flower-like serenity
that speaks of
care, reverence,

a thankful communion
with life's gifts of
sacred energy, awareness, time.

The weave of her russet dress
is shadowed,
glazed by light.

She meditates —
at the mercy and yet,
and yet,
utterly, enduringly, present.

3

The painter, a plastic surgeon
of the face and head –
knowing, therefore
all too well, how to read
the contours of malaise –

now gives us this reading
of beauty, of William Blake's
'the human form divine'

and we are invited
to contemplate how
     dance
is rooted in silence, stillness –

silence, a way of hearing the music that never stops
stillness, a way of hearing that silence

4

Once, so long ago,
I saw a dancer in performance
begin to shape
an arm movement,
a meditative arc,
more slowly, it seemed,
than the others around her

as if letting the lit air
carry her arm's weight,
yet completing that gesture,
that act of belief, first,
its grace vibrating
in now silent
space.

5

Once, so long ago,
two of us sat high on a hill
watching our friends dance below,
circling each other on the grass
wildly, yet as one.

When I said, with irony,
'We are up here,
looking down at the Dance of Life',
his response was:
'You can only see the Dance of Life
if you are in it.'

Dusk came,
the dancers danced on.

Shadows

To the caregivers, in a time of pandemic

I

St. Peter Healing the Sick with His Shadow by Masaccio

believers… brought forth the sick into the streets, and laid them on beds and couches,
that, at the least, the shadow of Peter passing by might overshadow some of them.
  – The Acts of the Apostles (5:12-14)

Masaccio,
the painter who first used light
to sculpt the human form,
portrayed this story.

The disciple, Peter,
walks through a Florentine street
past three afflicted men,
'the halt and the lame',

his shadow touching each in turn –
so that one man has already
raised himself, stands straight,
his hands in prayer-clasp,

the next, an old man
sparsely clothed as an eremite,
is halfway up,
his arms crossed on his breast,

the third,
who has lived an impossible life,
leans forward over his stick-like legs,
ready, with an awestruck look

to rise, any moment now,
to his full, unknown height.
Peter, his eyes bright with trance,
feet bare on the stones, moves on.

Masaccio, a fierce, benign,
wondrously gifted
unlocker of sacred secrets,
created this fresco, lit by

the Brancacci Chapel's great window
as he laboured, all-giving.
Three years later, aged twenty-six,
he would die in Rome. No details known.

II

Intensive Care: COVID-19

In the sealed unit,
among a paraphernalia of tubes
thick as aortas or thin as veins,
are those who tend minutely,

minute by minute,
the laceratingly ill —
in each bed, a human awareness
pulsing inside a racked body

until the turning that signals
recovery or death —
a sheet stretched upward
or, feet brought slowly down to earth.

The carers, the medical warriors,
have no time, no strength to fight
neglect by powerful others:
the tragic lack of ventilators,

of masks and visors
for the nurses, the doctors —
some fated to lie in beds
left by those they tended.

The shadows within this room,
watery grey or tinged with blue,
mere shadows of themselves,
cling to walls, floor, ceiling,

but shift, quicken
when carers draw near to read,
as they can, the charts and screens,
their patients' faces, vital signs.

If only, oh if only, such shadows
could do the work of healing for us,
reaching like an arm to comfort,
transmit the manna of our care,

and – in balance with the light,
in company with it – create
a deepened luminance,
as of a starred twilight

offering its presence
before darkness falls,
or a midwinter dawn
seeding itself from night –

liminal still,
while slowly lifting toward
a new day's flowering;
the whole room held in peace.

Easter, 2020

A Death in Winter

A Death in Winter

In Memory of Leo Seemanpillai
who died on June 1, 2014

   1

Let me, first, take my bearings
by speaking of weather, the season.

A spell of summer, late in autumn,
has lasted until this first day of winter,
will last beyond it.

I step outside, tilt my face up
to receive the sun.
Inside my closed eyes,
a canopy of sepia
tinged with cloudy gold;
as in a mica-flecked cave,
many star-points appear —
each a single flare, then gone.

   Soon my eyes — the eyes
   of my spirit, my deepest self —
   will hold the image of
   a burning man.

   On this day, at 9.15 a.m.,
   Leo Seemanpillai
   died in a Melbourne Hospital
   after an act of self-immolation.

2

I read the newspapers,
learn of Leo's life:
of how, when he was six,
his family fled from Sri Lanka
to a camp for refugees in India.

Returning as a young man to Sri Lanka
he was tortured by the military;
beaten by police and left to die.
Back in India, more persecution.
Then the journey to Australia –
en route, detention in Sumatra,
grave abuse and cruelty there.

In sum, a tidal wave of suffering
has broken over Leo Seemanpillai
and left him on an unlit shore.

Once here in Australia
he responds to others in need
with generosity, kindness,
turns his suffering into hope,
sows hope in others.

When, two days before his death,
a loved gift, a turquoise tile
painted with a butterfly, breaks,
he laughs it off.

3

Leo Seemanpillai arrived in Darwin from India on
January 9, 2013, and was held in detention before being
granted a bridging visa with work rights in June, 2013.

After he settles in Geelong
Leo, who knows English well,
may have seen the bumper stickers –
    They came. They saw. They sank.
But here he will find friendship,
enter the life of his community.

    In the week after Leo's death
    a workmate will speak of his keenness
    to do his job – one day a week
    cleaning trucks, mowing the lawn –
    and recall how he would
    lay out his uniform with care,
    finish his lunch break five minutes early
    to return to work.

4

Anyone who may have come from Sri Lanka should know
that they will go back to Sri Lanka.
– Scott Morrison, Minister for Immigration and Border Protection; October, 2013

A man on fire
is running from the front garden
of the house where he lived
into the street.

A neighbour who is a nurse
tries to help him.

Later that day, in a Melbourne hospital,
dying in agony,
he asks for his organs to be donated.

His parents, speaking from their refugee camp,
support his wishes.

Five people will benefit
from the gift of
an eye, both kidneys, his liver and one lung
from Leo Seemanpillai.

5

A man casts off and rows
across a lake of fire
in the small boat of his body

because he feels, because
everything he knows now tells him,
that he can do no other.

This last act of torture
that will end all torture.

6

How can I venture
to speak of such things?

I step back now,
insist that I do not know
what Leo's sufferings might have been like.

I can only create –
for myself, for others –
a space for imagining.

7

A friend rings from England.
Of the terrifying mayhem
that is now, (again), Iraq,
she says:
    'When we can see no clear way forward,
    no way to offer help or hope,
    the way forward
    is to travel within
    and dwell inside the cave of stillness.
    There will be found the peace we can offer.'

But here, now, in Australia
new choices can be made,
bad decisions reversed,
so that the tortured, the persecuted,
will not be sent back to the hellholes –
old ones, new ones –
where persecutors hold sway.

8

If I'm deported back to Sri Lanka, torture is certain
because I'm a Tamil.
   − from the Journal of Leo Seemanpillai

In a meditation class
I take to heart these words:
   Be aware of each breath, treasure it.
   You will never have this breath again.

I have started to imagine
all the breaths Leo might have had,
the days and years he might have had,
and the kindness friends and others
would have known from him,
and he from them.

9

Leo had, pinned to his wall, a slip of paper that read,
It is our light, not our darkness, that most frightens us.

Leo, one of the light-bearers,
had reason, though, to fear the dark.

After a friend gave him a night-light
to help him sleep, he told her

it was like 'a shiny moon'
always there inside his room.

10

I watch a mica-cloud of midges
above the winter sun –
small winter suns themselves,
their shaped flux set against
that far-off cypress.

I think of sky-loving murmurations,
of spaces within the mind, the heart,
drawn tightly close
then flowing outwards, oceanic,
within a split second.

When I look up again
the clouds are seamed with chrysolite;
no sun; the air blank.

11

During a stay in a Mental Hospital early in 2014 because of
severe depression, Leo tried to hang himself with a towel.

Who, exactly, is ill here?

Doctors sometimes forsake
medical language, to speak of
heart murmurs, shadows on a lung.

We live now with fear,
its murmurs, its shadows,
carried in the heart, the lungs:

the fear of losing —
even of sharing —
the smallest part of what we possess.

Some of us have
plighted our troth with fear:

in the caves of the heart, the lungs,
loving our fear.

It is time to breathe freely, to feel.

12

On the day I hear of Leo's death
I pass a tall maple,
its star-like leaves, blood-red
and flame-red, irradiated.

Many leaves have fallen,
many leaves still pattern the air;
all will be gone by the Solstice.

Tree of fire, tree of blood.

13

I walk the cliff path
under a cloud-marbled white dome —
having just missed, I'm told,
two sea-eagles flying around the bay,
their eyes reading its waters.

Back home I listen to Early Choral music
that has echoed inside cathedral domes,
caves of light mixed with incense,
each note a mica glint
ascending into the light beyond the light we see —
a further light
that presses back on us.

We live,
sub specie aeternitatis —
'under the aspect of eternity'

14

We get to listen to the silence in the cave,
and perhaps we can even hear our own heartbeats.
    — Werner Herzog

And now I watch
Herzog's *Cave of Forgotten Dreams* —
a film that takes me inside the Chauvet Cave:
sealed by a rockslide for twenty thousand years,
newly discovered.
A raised light presses into the darkness
and that ancient darkness,
pricked with mica glints,
presses back against the light.
There are scratches from bear claws
on walls painted with horses,
wild and strange,
in the mystery of their nature,
the light in their eyes
preserved through thirty millennia.

And, among bones on the floor of the Cave —
the province now of archaeologists,
forensic scientists —
the skeleton of a golden eagle.

Outside, in this present world,
and less than twenty miles from Chauvet Cave,
run-off from a nuclear power plant
feeds toxic lagoons where crocodiles
multiply, mutate.
A white crocodile with white eyes
curves up to the surface, to breathe.

15

Spirit of Life
may you guard the afflicted,
    those who have suffered
    beyond reason, beyond imagining,
    those who fear certain persecution —
may a haven be found for them
somewhere this side of death.

Spirit of Life
save us from the white crocodiles.

16

Some speak of
the solace of eternity

some believe that in death
we become part of everything,
our spark of awareness
carried by all the winds that blow
then above them
into the light beyond light.

May Leo
rest in peace

May his mother and father, his brothers,
know peace

May the many people here who loved him
know peace.

17

We want to be by our son's side when his funeral takes place.
That way our lives will be more peaceful.
  — Leo's father

The Australian government refused the visas applied for
by Leo's family so that they might attend his funeral.

As three Tamil men at a microphone
sing a long hymn in Tamil
the Basilica fills with an undertow of sound,

a faint bass humming by many voices
that I cannot account for until, at the end,
Leo's coffin is carried out
followed by a procession of Tamil men
who'd sat, unseen by me, at the front.
They carry their bodies, their spirits, so quietly.
Some of them, I know,
have cigarette burns on their backs
and other scars.

We all wait in the silver light.

It is achieved.

The funeral car starts its slow journey.

The elderly woman I'd sat beside,
who had travelled three hours to be here,
turns down my offer of a lift,
chooses, despite her damaged leg,
to walk with her stroller
to the railway station.

   'It'll be thinking time,' she says,
   calmly passionate.
   'There is a lot to think about.'

Notes

Notes

Most of the paintings, photographs and poems alluded to in various poems can be accessed on the internet.

'Blackout'

New York Movie, 1939, by Edward Hopper.
The waterfalls of the Iguazu River, on the border of Argentina and Brazil, make up the largest waterfall in the world. The Devil's Throat is a chasm set within it, curtained by fourteen falls. The water of the lower Iguazu collects in a canyon that drains into the Paraná River.

'Unearthly'

See photographs by Alexander Gerst on thisiscolossal.com: 'Clouds Cast Thousand-Mile Shadows into Space When Viewed Aboard the International Space Station' by Christopher Jobson, September 1, 2014.

'Midsummer'

'The Infinite a sudden Guest' is poem 1309 in *The Complete Poems of Emily Dickinson,* ed. Thomas H. Johnson. Clifton Springs, a town on the Bellarine Peninsula, in Victoria, overlooks Corio Bay and the You Yangs mountain range.

'Anniversary Visit'

The reference in line 6 is to Diane Fahey's poetry collection, *A House by the River.*

'Bowers'

'Forever — is composed of Nows — ' begins poem 624, and the phrase 'Blue Peninsula' appears in 'It might be lonelier', poem 405, in *The Complete Poems of Emily Dickinson,* ed. Thomas H. Johnson.

'Glass Flowers'

Paintings from Dena Kahan's *Glass Garden* series can be viewed on
denakahan.com. *Glass Garden #3* is the key work focused upon in this
sequence, in particular that part of it which forms the subject of *Glass
Garden #14*: the latter can be accessed separately on the internet. The
paintings are based on the *Glass Flowers* exhibit at Harvard Museum of
Natural History, which displays botanical studies made by Leopold and
Rudolf Blaschka from 1887 through to 1936: hmnh.harvard.edu

'The Yellow Room'

'The Yellow Room' is based on *The Chinese Screen*, 1995, one of the
paintings by Margaret Olley featuring the often-painted subject of
the yellow room, some with the inclusion of a screen. The painting in
question may not be accessible online but a similar one, *Chinese Screen
and Yellow Room*, 1996, is: artgallery.nsw.gov.au. See also: *Yellow Room
with Chinese Screen*, 1995, at 'The Olley Project' on ehive.com. The main
variants are the painting on the right wall (in *The Chinese Screen*, it is
Dance (1) by Henri Matisse), and the objects on the table.

'Face'

Portrait in the mirror, 1948, can be found on artgallery.nsw.gov.au
Dressing table (self portrait), 1982, painted after the death of Margaret
Olley's mother, is held in a private collection but can be accessed on the
internet.

'The Black Cockatoos'

On leilajeffreys.com, see 'Biloela Wild Cockatoos, exhibited 2012'.
The film, *Bird Nerd: the Art of Leila Jeffreys*, provided valuable material
for this poem.

'Portraiture'

A number of online sites contain selections of Eugène Atget's photographs, including atgetphotography.com. The photographs cited can be directly accessed by their titles. Examples of Atget's photographs of Squares, are: *Pontoise, Place du Grand-Martroy*, 1902, *Place du Tertre*, 1922, and *Montmartre, Place du Tertre*, 1924.

'At Niagara Galleries'

The paintings cited below are the main sources for the themes and images alluded to in 'At Niagara Galleries' — some of these also appear in other works by Rick Amor. Many of the paintings can be found on the internet. See also: catalogue.rickamor.com.au

1. Small study for *A dream of the sea* 1998, and *Shark in a wave* 2002; *The bay* 2003 and *The bay at evening* 2005; *The terminal* 2017; *By the long sea* 1995, *Silent east II* 2006, and *The ship* 2006; *The runner* 1988; *Out to sea* 1993; *Evening on Long Island, Victoria* 1995-97; *Town by the sea* 1989-90, and *A town by the sea (looking back)* 1990

2. *The Outlying Districts* 2001-2; *Burning car* 1997, and *Near the East River* 1998; *Entering the city* 2006

3. *The empty days* 1998; *The quiet days* 1998-99

4. An image of *The Room (Memory)*, 1994, can be accessed directly on the internet, and on portrait.gov.au/'Rick Amor, 21 Portraits'.

5. 'the outlying districts'. A number of works by Rick Amor draw on this theme, presenting liminal wastelands, derelict monumental structures, and major building or bridge works in progress outside the inner city.

'The Postcard'

Rick Amor's *Self-portrait with postcard of Greco Roman bust*, 2003, is held in The University of Queensland Art Collection: art-museum.uq.edu.au 'cliffs of fall' appears in Gerard Manley Hopkins' sonnet, 'No worst, there is none. Pitched past pitch of grief', in the lines: 'O the mind, mind has mountains; cliffs of fall / Frightful, sheer, no-man-fathomed.'

'The Room'

Ragianna Bird-of-Paradise and *Blue Bird-of-Paradise* by Ellis Rowan, *Bedfordia Salicina* and *Richea Milliganii* by Margaret Stones, a study for *Glass Garden #14* by Dena Kahan, *Poppies in a Glass Jar* by Margaret Olley, *The Red Boat* by Clarice Beckett. Rick Amor's *Street at Night* is archived on catalogue.rickamor.com.au

'Flight to the Stars'

Tjungkara Ken's *Kungkarangkalpa tjukurpa (Seven Sisters dreaming), a self-portrait*, is included, with information on the artist, in the section on The Archibald Prize for 2017, artgallery.nsw.gov.au, which includes these recorded words of Tjungkara Ken:
'When the ancestors painted our tjukurpa (dreaming) on the caves and on their bodies, it was a celebration of our culture, a way of identifying people and places, and a way of continuing our stories. Today, we have new materials and ways but the celebration and commitment to tjukurpa and cultural identity is always the same.'

'Shimmer'

Ms. G (Djotarra) Yunupingu was a Yolŋu artist who belonged to the Yirrkala Community in North East Arnhem Land. Her life and work as an artist have been written about in a Profile on cooeeart.com.au, in 2012, and in the Obituary by Will Stubbs on artlink.com.au, June 2013. I am indebted to these sources, and to the Obituary by Jeremy Eccles in *The Sydney Morning Herald*, June 13, 2012, from which the first quotation beneath the title of 'Shimmer' is taken. The second quotation beneath the title, and the following quotation, are from Georges Petitjean's *Contemporary Aboriginal Art*:
'Yolŋu artists stress that the process of painting is a religious act and that the vibrancy of the painted surface is a manifestation of ancestral power.'

'Dancer'

The inner stillness of Eileen Kramer by Andrew Lloyd Greensmith is
included, with information on Eileen Kramer and on the artist, in the
section on The Archibald Prize for 2017, artgallery.nsw.gov.au
'the human form divine' is from William Blake's poem, 'The Divine Image'.

'Shadows'

Masaccio is considered to have begun the Early Italian Renaissance
in painting. The fresco, *Holy Trinity*, is commonly held to be his
masterwork.

'A Death in Winter'

For background material about Leo Seemanpillai, see, for instance, the
articles by Konrad Marshall, (June 17, 2014), and Nick Toscano, (June 18,
2014), in *The Sydney Morning Herald*, archived on smh.com.au
In section 3, the term 'bridging visa' is used. Leo Seemanpillai was
not given a refugee visa by the Australian Government's Department
of Home Affairs, but rather a temporary visa with no certain path to
permanent residency: 'With this visa [Bridging visa A] you can... stay
lawfully in Australia until your substantive visa application [also
temporary] is finally determined... A BVA will end immediately if... we
cancel either your BVA or the substantive visa that you held when you
were granted the BVA.'
In the final section, *'It is achieved'* alludes to the sacrificial death of Jesus,
in the *Gospel of John*, 19:30. 'After he took the wine, Jesus said, "It's
done... complete." Bowing his head, he offered up his spirit.'

Acknowledgements

Various poems have appeared in the following print and online publications:

'Blackout' in *Meanjin*, 2021

'Autumn Begins' in *Meanjin*, 2020

'A History of the Lotus', 'Zen Morning' and 'At the Solstice' in *Eureka Street*: eurekastreet.com.au

'Late Spring Gardens' and 'Introit' in *Anthropocene*, 2021: anthropocenepoetry.org

'Garden Walk, Daybreak' and 'In Winter Light' in *World Poetry Journal*, 2021

'The Unquiet Garden' in *Tinteán*, 2021: tintean.org.au

'Visitations' in *Porridge Magazine*, 2021: porridgemagazine.com

'Anniversary Visit' in *Live Encounters Poetry & Writing*, 2018: liveencounters.net

'Glass Flowers' in the exhibition catalogue of Dena Kahan's *The Glass Garden* (Art Gallery of Ballarat, 2015); excerpts from it appear in *Cordite*, 2017: cordite.org.au

'The Yellow Room' in *The Ekphrastic Review*, 2021: ekphrastic.net

'In Half Light', (the retitled third section of 'Face'), in *Not Very Quiet*, 2021: not-very-quiet.com

'The Black Cockatoos' in *Cordite*, 2020: cordite.org.au

'The Square' (from 'Portraiture') in *The Montreal Poetry Prize Anthology 2020*

'Rooms by the Sea' in *Irises: The University of Canberra Vice-Chancellor's International Poetry Prize 2017*

'Shimmer' in *Antipodes*, 2019

'Dancer' and 'Shadows' in eurekastreet.com.au

'A Death in Winter' in *Index on Censorship*, 2014, and eurekastreet.com.au; excerpts included in the anthology *Writing to the Wire* (UWA publishing, 2016)

Individual poems by Diane Fahey were shortlisted for the Montreal Poetry Prize, 2020, and the Fish Poetry Prize, 2019, with long listings for the Peter Porter Poetry Prize, 2019, and the University of Canberra Vice-Chancellor's International Poetry Prize, 2017.

*

My warm thanks to the family of Ms. G (Djotarra) Yunupingu for permission to refer to her life story in 'Shimmer'.

*

My warm thanks to Dena Kahan for permission to reproduce part of *Large Glass Garden #2* on the cover of *Glass Flowers*.

*

I live and write on Wadawurrung Country, and acknowledge the Traditional Custodians, past, present and future, of this place.

www.ingramcontent.com/pod-product-compliance
Lightning Source LLC
Chambersburg PA
CBHW030942090426
42737CB00007B/503